Hal•Leonard
INSTRUMENTAL
PLAY-ALONG

AUDIO
ACCESS
INCLUDED

PLAYBACK+
Speed • Pitch • Balance • Loop

Flute

Jazz Blues Favorites

Audio arrangements by Peter Deneff

To access audio visit:
www.halleonard.com/mylibrary

Enter Code
3574-4413-7522-1579

ISBN 978-1-4950-5335-1

Hal•Leonard®

7777 W. BLUEMOUND RD. P.O. BOX 13819 MILWAUKEE, WI 53213

Visit Hal Leonard Online at
www.halleonard.com

ALL BLUES

flute

By MILES DAVIS

BASIN STREET BLUES

FLUTE

Words and Music by
SPENCER WILLIAMS

BIRK'S WORKS

Flute

By DIZZY GILLESPIE

C-JAM BLUES

Flute

By DUKE ELLINGTON

FREDDIE FREELOADER

Flute

By MILES DAVIS

MR. P.C.

FLUTE

By JOHN COLTRANE

NIGHT TRAIN

Flute

Words by OSCAR WASHINGTON
and LEWIS C. SIMPKINS
Music by JIMMY FORREST

NOW'S THE TIME

Flute

By CHARLIE PARKER

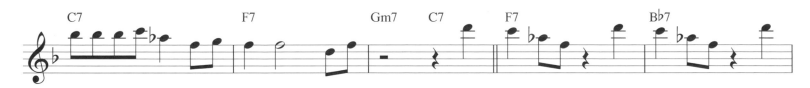

ONE FOR DADDY-O

Flute

By NAT ADDERLY

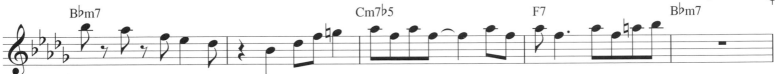

THE SWINGIN' SHEPHERD BLUES

flute

Words and Music by MOE KOFFMAN,
RHODA ROBERTS and KENNY JACOBSON

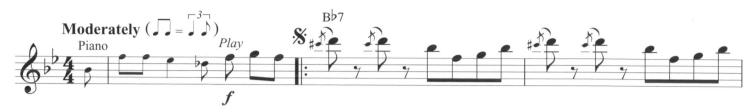

TENOR MADNESS

Flute

By SONNY ROLLINS

THINGS AIN'T WHAT THEY USED TO BE

Flute

By MERCER ELLINGTON

101 SONGS

YOUR FAVORITE SONGS ARE ARRANGED FOR SOLO INSTRUMENTALISTS WITH THIS GREAT SERIES.

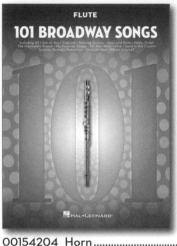

FLUTE
101 BROADWAY SONGS

101 BROADWAY SONGS

Cabaret • Do You Hear the People Sing? • Edelweiss • Guys and Dolls • Hello, Dolly! • I Dreamed a Dream • If I Were a Bell • Luck Be a Lady • Ol' Man River • Seasons of Love • Send in the Clowns • Think of Me • Tomorrow • What I Did for Love • and many more.

00154199	Flute	$14.99
00154200	Clarinet	$14.99
00154201	Alto Sax	$14.99
00154202	Tenor Sax	$14.99
00154203	Trumpet	$14.99
00154204	Horn	$14.99
00154205	Trombone	$14.99
00154206	Violin	$14.99
00154207	Viola	$14.99
00154208	Cello	$14.99

CELLO
101 HIT SONGS

101 HIT SONGS

All About That Bass • All of Me • Brave • Breakaway • Clocks • Fields of Gold • Firework • Hey, Soul Sister • Ho Hey • I Gotta Feeling • Jar of Hearts • Love Story • 100 Years • Roar • Rolling in the Deep • Shake It Off • Smells like Teen Spirit • Uptown Funk • and more.

00194561	Flute	$16.99
00197182	Clarinet	$16.99
00197183	Alto Sax	$16.99
00197184	Tenor Sax	$16.99
00197185	Trumpet	$16.99
00197186	Horn	$16.99
00197187	Trombone	$16.99
00197188	Violin	$16.99
00197189	Viola	$16.99
00197190	Cello	$16.99

VIOLIN
101 CLASSICAL THEMES

101 CLASSICAL THEMES

Ave Maria • Bist du bei mir (You Are with Me) • Canon in D • Clair de Lune • Dance of the Sugar Plum Fairy • 1812 Overture • Eine Kleine Nachtmusik ("Serenade"), First Movement Excerpt • The Flight of the Bumble Bee • Funeral March of a Marionette • Fur Elise • Gymnopedie No. 1 • Jesu, Joy of Man's Desiring • Lullaby • Minuet in G • Ode to Joy • Piano Sonata in C • Pie Jesu • Rondeau • Theme from Swan Lake • Wedding March • William Tell Overture • and many more.

00155315	Flute	$14.99
00155317	Clarinet	$14.99
00155318	Alto Sax	$14.99
00155319	Tenor Sax	$14.99
00155320	Trumpet	$14.99
00155321	Horn	$14.99
00155322	Trombone	$14.99
00155323	Violin	$14.99
00155324	Viola	$14.99
00155325	Cello	$14.99

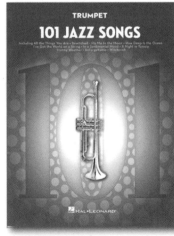

TRUMPET
101 JAZZ SONGS

101 JAZZ SONGS

All of Me • Autumn Leaves • Bewitched • Blue Skies • Body and Soul • Cheek to Cheek • Come Rain or Come Shine • Don't Get Around Much Anymore • A Fine Romance • Here's to Life • I Could Write a Book • It Could Happen to You • The Lady Is a Tramp • Like Someone in Love • Lullaby of Birdland • The Nearness of You • On Green Dolphin Street • Satin Doll • Stella by Starlight • Tangerine • Unforgettable • The Way You Look Tonight • Yesterdays • and many more.

00146363	Flute	$14.99
00146364	Clarinet	$14.99
00146366	Alto Sax	$14.99
00146367	Tenor Sax	$14.99
00146368	Trumpet	$14.99
00146369	Horn	$14.99
00146370	Trombone	$14.99
00146371	Violin	$14.99
00146372	Viola	$14.99
00146373	Cello	$14.99

HAL•LEONARD®

www.halleonard.com

Prices, contents and availability subject to change without notice.

0217